The Happiness Book For Kids

A Kid's Guide To Happiness!
Volume II

Mike Duffy

ISBN-13:978-0692331842
ISBN-10:0692331840

DEDICATION

I dedicate this book to my incredible family including my beautiful wife Shannon, my gorgeous daughter, Kendall and my wonderful son, Michael

Feeling happy is fantastic! In this book you will learn the secrets to happiness. Try one every day. These secrets will give you a lifetime of joy and happiness!

Love

Love is the most important part of life. Love is why we are here. Love everybody. We all need love to live. Love deeply, bravely, and generously and I promise that you will be happy!

Share

Share your toys with a friend. Share your snacks with a brother or a sister. When you share with someone, they'll share with you.

Listen

When you are at school, listen to the teachers. When you are at home, listen to your parents. It's important to hear people that care about you.

Relax

Take time to unwind from a busy day. Lay back and think of all the great things that happened. Your wonderful body needs to rest.

Play

Life is fun! Go outside with an adult and a friend and go bananas! Play hopscotch, soccer, and tag or even make up a new game.

Make New Friends.

One of life's best treats is a friend. They share your secrets. They make new great memories with you. There is a whole world of friends that you haven't met yet. When you see someone that you would like to make friends with say, "Hi my name is _____. What's yours?"

Enjoy Right Now

Always live in the moment. Be present to what is going on around you. This great life moves fast. Don't wait to be happy.

Learn

Learning is fun! Learn as much as you can everyday. Learning makes you smarter!

Watch Happy Shows

Your brain is like a computer. If you program your brain with happy TV shows and movies, you'll feel happier. Funny movies make you feel good!

Dance

Let it all hang out on the dance floor! The whole world is your dance floor. Make up silly dances that make your friends laugh.

Do good deeds

Set the table before dinner. Make your parents a card that has a picture of your family on it. Volunteer to help someone. Believe it or not, you'll be the one who feels that happiest as a result of your good deeds!

Think

Use your incredible brain to work out your problems. There is always a solution to every problem. Take the time to think of ways to succeed. You can do it!

Imagine

Your imagination is powerful! Use your imagination to go on fantastic journeys in far away lands. Imagine what it would be like to fly. You can go anywhere and do anything using your imagination.

Listen To Happy Music

Happy music gets your toes tapping, your head shaking and your smile going. Happy music fills your soul with energy. It puts you in a great mood!

Memorize A Joke

Everyone loves a good joke. A good joke is a great present that you can give someone else. Here's a silly joke for you:

Why was 6 afraid of 7? Because 7 ate 9!

Sing

Sing along with your favorite song. Sing with a friend. Sing out loud! Make up a funny song or change the words to a song for great laughs.

Play Sports

Sports are great exercise. You learn how to be a good teammate and make friends as well. Softball, soccer, hockey, basketball, swimming, ice-skating and volleyball are just some of the sports that you should try!

Play An Instrument

Playing an instrument is cool! You can create so many different sounds. You can join a band and make music with friends. You can rock out and make people dance!

Say Sorry

We all make mistakes. When you hurt someone, tell the person that you are sorry. That way, they can forgive you and it will make them feel better.

Draw

Want to see a pirate's treasure map? Draw it! Your imagination loves to have your fingers show what it is thinking on paper. Feel free to draw anything in and outside of this universe. Draw a bulldog. Make sure you don't draw on the walls!

Ask For Help

Adults are happy to help kids. It makes them feel good. If you are having a problem, ask a parent to help you.

Dream

Dream what it will be like inventing the next big thing. Dream how you will feel making other people's lives better as a result of you helping them. Dreams are movies that you produce, star in and direct in your head. Dream big!

Do Not Be Afraid

Fear is the enemy of happiness. You cannot be happy and afraid at the same time. Choose to be happy instead of being afraid. Think of life as one big, happy adventure!

About the Author

Mike Duffy is the founder of Happiness Publishing, LLC. He has been researching happiness for over 29 years. He is the author of *The Happiness Book For Kids: A Kid's Guide To Happiness! Volume I & II, The Happiness Book For Little Christians: A Biblical Guide To Happiness!* and *The Happiness Book For Men: A Man's Guide To Happiness.* He loves to speak about how you can gain greater happiness and joy in your wonderful and precious life. His audiences include corporations, universities and organizations. Mike is the founder of The Happiness Hall Of Fame. The Happiness Hall of Fame recognizes, encourages and celebrates people that through their talent, hard work and sacrifice make other people happy.
www.happinesshalloffame.com

Credits

All of the wonderful photos are from
123 RF.com. A great thank you to the following
artists:
John McAllister© *123RF.com*
Liliya Kulianionak© *123RF.com*
damedeeso© *123RF.com*
Tatiana Katsia© *123RF.com*
Denis Aglichev© *123RF.com*
Robert Neumann© *123RF.com*
ewastudio© *123RF.com*
Tammy McAllister© *123RF.com*
Narinnate Mekkajorn© *123RF.com*

Acknowledgements

I would like to thank all of the people that have shared their wisdom with me including: Dr. Fred Luskin, Dr. Laura Delizonna, Deepak Chopra, Tal Ben-Shahar, Shawn Achor, Dan Gilbert, Deepak Chopra and Zelig Pliskin.

www.ingramcontent.com/pod-product-compliance
Lightning Source LLC
LaVergne TN
LVHW010023070426
835508LV00001B/16